For more than forty years,
Yearling has been the leading name
in classic and award-winning literature
for young readers.

Yearling books feature children's
favorite authors and characters,
providing dynamic stories of adventure,
humor, history, mystery, and fantasy.

Trust Yearling paperbacks to entertain,
inspire, and promote the love of reading
in all children.

BOOKS BY JOAN LOWERY NIXON

Mysteries

A Candidate for Murder
The Dark and Deadly Pool
A Deadly Game of Magic
Don't Scream
The Ghosts of Now
Ghost Town
The Haunting
The Kidnapping of Christina Lattimore
Laugh Till You Cry
Murdered, My Sweet
The Name of the Game Was Murder
Nightmare
Nobody's There
The Other Side of Dark
Playing for Keeps
Search for the Shadowman
Secret, Silent Screams
Shadowmaker
The Specter
Spirit Seeker
The Stalker
The Trap
The Weekend Was Murder!
Whispers from the Dead
Who Are You?

Series

ELLIS ISLAND
Land of Hope

THE ORPHAN TRAIN ADVENTURES
Caught in the Act
A Dangerous Promise
A Family Apart
In the Face of Danger
A Place to Belong

OTHER YEARLING BOOKS YOU WILL ENJOY

THE DARK AND DEADLY POOL, *Joan Lowery Nixon*

THE HAUNTING, *Joan Lowery Nixon*

MURDERED, MY SWEET, *Joan Lowery Nixon*

THE EGYPT GAME, *Zilpha Keatley Snyder*

HARRIET THE SPY®, *Louise Fitzhugh*

THE FARTHEST-AWAY MOUNTAIN, *Lynne Reid Banks*

CLUES IN THE WOODS, *Peggy Parish*

MIDWINTER NIGHTINGALE, *Joan Aiken*

THE WORRY WEB SITE, *Jacqueline Wilson*

THE GHOST IN THE BIG BRASS BED, *Bruce Coville*

Joan Lowery Nixon

The Making of a Writer

A YEARLING BOOK

Published by Yearling, an imprint of Random House Children's Books
a division of Random House, Inc., New York

Yearling and the jumping horse design are registered trademarks of Random House, Inc.

Visit us on the Web! www.randomhouse.com/kids

Educators and librarians, for a variety of teaching tools, visit us at
www.randomhouse.com/teachers

ISBN: 0-440-41905-0

Reprinted by arrangement with Delacorte Press

Printed in the United States of America

September 2003

10 9 8 7 6 5 4 3

OPM

For Pat,
whom I cherish

The Making
of a Writer

Introduction

You love to read. You love to write. Many of you have written to me to ask, "How can I become a published writer someday?"

My answers to your letters often include the advice to read, read, read. A love of reading leads to a love of writing.

I also suggest that you write for your own pleasure every chance you get. In some letters I've explained the importance of character development. In others I've suggested ways to make story beginnings exciting. I always try to help you understand the *process* of creating a story.

Writing is much more than learning a few rules from a necessarily short letter. Writing is a complicated mixture of talent, art, craft, structure, free-flowing ideas, unleashed imagination, soaring hopes, wondrous insights, giddy joy, deep satisfaction, dreadful insecurity, total misery, strong persistence, and solid determination.

Writing is an ever-developing awareness of people and events that has its beginnings in childhood.

At some point nearly every writer takes stock of a lifetime of accumulated experiences. Sometimes it's surprising to discover the writer's special awareness, which began in the early years and has subtly guided the direction that person has taken.

This book is about the incidents that happened when I was young that helped me grow and develop as a writer.

I hope that what I share with you will not only entertain you, but will also lead you to keep your eyes and ears open to the insights and ideas that will come bursting into your own imagination.

Happy reading. Happy writing—now and in the future.

Chapter One

When I was young I filled notebooks with my writing. Sometimes I jotted down special thoughts, bits of description, verses, and short stories.

The number of greeting cards I designed, with personalized verses inside, would have shaken the marketing department heads of Hallmark. Every member of my family received my illustrated poems on holidays, birthdays, other special occasions, and sometimes just-for-fun days. It made my relatives and friends feel special, and I suppose it also saved me money at the greeting card store.

When I was ten, I mailed one of my poems to a children's magazine to which I subscribed. I can't remember the name of the magazine, but it had a page devoted to children's writing and art.

My poem was titled "Springtime," and I remember that one line was "and children play outdoors because they're glad it's spring." There must have been some literary license involved because in Los Angeles children played outdoors all year round.

In April 1938, two months after my eleventh birthday, I opened the just-arrived issue of the magazine. There on the children's page was my printed poem, with the byline *Joan Lowery, age 10.*

My name! My byline! In a magazine that people all over the United States would read!

I can still visualize my name in print under the words I had written. This was what it was like to be a published writer. In print! With a byline! Delirious with success, I knew I was on my way.

Chapter Two

When I was a baby my parents and my mother's parents, Mathias (Matt) and Harriet (Hattie) Meyer, whom we called Nanny and Pa, bought a white stucco duplex on the corner of 73rd Street and Gramercy in Los Angeles. They added a large, square room that connected the two sides of the house through my parents' and grandparents' dining rooms. Since my mother had been a kindergarten teacher, the room was outfitted like her former classroom with an upright piano, a sturdy work table and chairs, easels and poster paints, a school-sized blackboard, a ceramic pot that held damp clay, a dollhouse, and a roomy space for toys. Everyone called it the playroom.

My parents' side of the house was arranged in a square, and my grandparents' side of the house was shaped like an upside-down *L*. After my sister Pat was born, when I was five, she and my other younger sister, Marilyn, shared the second bedroom in our parents' side of the house. My bedroom was on my grandparents' side of the house, at the far end of the upside-down *L*.

The two sides of the house were quite different, although both had chairs and sofas upholstered in the stiff, prickly plush fabric that was in fashion then. I can't remember what color they were because they were all covered in homemade slipcovers of printed fabric that didn't match but had been purchased at a "good bargain." The object was to protect the furniture underneath. The slipcovers were removed only for special guests and parties at which there would be no children.

I can see now that the slipcovers cut out a lot of the stress to which children are subjected. With the furniture well protected, no one cared if we climbed onto the sofa with our shoes on to color the designs in our coloring books, or sat there munching on saltine crackers.

The gas stove in my mother's kitchen was fairly new. It looked like a table on white enameled iron legs with the oven on top, next to the four burners. Nanny had an old, heavy iron stove whose oven was like a dark cavern underneath the burners. Mother had an electric refrigerator, but Nanny had a wooden icebox out on the service porch.

Two times a week the iceman arrived in his truck, picked up a huge block of ice with tongs, and carried it on his back to replace the melted ice in the icebox. There was a pan underneath into which the melting ice could drip, and Pa had to empty this heavy pan at least once a day.

The children in the neighborhood loved to jump into the open back of the ice truck, grab slivers of ice, and run before the iceman returned. If he came back too soon, this good-natured man would pretend to scowl. He'd shout, "Who's taking my ice?" and then take a few steps toward us as we ran away squealing.

Nanny loved to cook and to bake, so both sides of the house were rich with the fragrances of pot roast and onions, cinnamon-sugar cookies, rich chocolate puddings, and comforting chicken soups.

Our grandparents and their activities played a big part in our lives.

Each spring Nanny and Pa bottled their own root beer. We all loved root beer, especially in black cows, sodas made of vanilla ice cream and root beer. Nanny cooked the root beer mixture and scalded the bottles, and after the brew had been poured into the bottles, Pa would cap them with a small metal bottle-capping tool that could be operated only by exerting great physical strength.

The bottles would be stored on the service porch, and after a certain period had passed in which the carbonation did its work, the root beer would be ready to drink.

It was delicious, and to add to the fun and excitement of each summer, every now and then a bottle on the service porch would explode with a noise we could hear all over the house.

It was best when I was young and could scream at the explosions. When I grew a little older I often had to help clean up the sticky mess.

I watched Nanny make fudge, which, at an exact time in its cooling, Pa, with his strong arm, beat into a creamy texture. Nanny taught me how to darn socks and took me with her when she visited her circle of friends in the neighborhood. Mrs. Christiana offered me cookies. Mrs. Ritemeyer, who subscribed to the *Los Angeles Times*'s rival newspaper, the *Examiner,* always saved her Sunday comics for me.

Nanny and Pa were wonderful companions and the best of baby-sitters. Tall, quiet Pa and chatty Nanny, who barely reached five feet tall, were infinitely patient and spent hours playing Chinese checkers, whist, and poker with us as we graduated from our early years of fish and slapjack. With both parents and grandparents close at hand, my sisters and I were tucked into a snug, secure environment.

In some of my earliest memories I see myself running to my grandfather and saying, "Pa, will you read to me?"

Pa, a sun-browned man with curly, graying hair, had retired from his job as a mail carrier. I could usually find him reading in his favorite armchair because he dearly loved good books. When I appeared, carrying as many picture books as I could hold, he'd close his own book in the middle of a sentence. He'd wait until I'd climbed up in his lap; then he'd begin reading.

Mother, who also loved to read, shared countless books with me, and later with my younger sisters, Marilyn and Pat. After I was grown Mother liked to remind me that before I was old enough to read or write, I'd sometimes come to her and say, "I have a poem, Mama. Write it down."

Apparently, from a very early age I understood that words could be put together in a wonderful way, then written down and kept forever. Even before I was old enough to begin gathering memories, I wanted to be a part of this writing-and-keeping process.

When I was young we didn't have television. It hadn't been invented. No one had dreamed up the Internet or electronic games to keep us solitarily indoors, so—unless it was raining—all the kids in the neighborhood got together outside and played red light–green light, hopscotch, hide-and-seek, and tag.

Adults had not yet organized kids into regulated teams for sports, so we made up our own. Occasionally, when conditions were right, we enjoyed a weed fight in the vacant lot in back of our house.

A perfect weed fight had to take place after a rain, when the dirt was loose and muddy. It was also important—for obvious reasons—that neither of my parents be at home. As all the neighborhood kids gathered in the lot, we'd choose sides and form teams. Then we'd grab handfuls of the tall grasses that covered the field, their roots tangled in balls of damp earth, and let fly.

It was great fun to throw dirt clods at each other until we were exhausted. The clods weren't hard enough to cause any damage, and no team actually won or lost the game. We simply ended up sweaty and itching, with dirt in our hair and ears and sifting down the necks of our shirts.

In our neighborhood we often played outside until just before dinner. Then we all dashed to our own homes so that we wouldn't miss the fifteen-minute radio dramas designed just for kids: *Jack Armstrong: the All-American Boy, Little Orphan Annie,* and *Uncle Whoa Bill,* a local children's talent program heard in the Los Angeles area.

But my very favorite radio program, the one I couldn't bear to miss, was *The Lone Ranger.* It came on at seven-thirty in the evening. As the Lone Ranger and his "faithful sidekick," Tonto, raced through canyons and across plains in their urgency to make the West safe for humanity, I could close my eyes and envision broad vistas of sun-scorched earth, glowing campfires, and dark night skies swept with glittering, oversized stars. In my mind the bad guys looked as mean as their voices, and I was sure that the settlers who were helped by the Lone Ranger had grateful, happy expressions on their upturned, trusting faces. The bad guys always lost, and the good guys—with the help of the Lone Ranger—always won. It was a comfortable world and satisfied my sense of justice.

My father, Joseph Lowery, an accountant, had an orderly, disciplined mind. When I was seven and school began again in September, he informed me that good students always got plenty of sleep. Therefore my bedtime on school nights would be at seven-thirty, not a minute later.

"Not seven-thirty!" I complained. "That's when *The Lone Ranger* comes on!"

Daddy was adamant. "Bedtime must be the same each night," he insisted. "Your routine shouldn't be interrupted by something as unimportant as a radio program."

"*The Lone Ranger is* important," I insisted, but my arguments didn't help. Tearfully, I obeyed, and Mother tucked me into bed exactly one minute before seven-thirty.

I didn't have long to feel sorry for myself. Suddenly the power of the theme music, the *William Tell Overture,* swirled through the room, and the familiar voice of the announcer began: "A fiery horse with the speed of light, a cloud of dust, and a hearty, 'Hi-Yo, Silver!' The Lone Ranger rides again."

In her living room at the front of the house, Nanny had turned the volume of their radio high enough that I could hear my favorite program in my back bedroom.

It didn't take long for Daddy to knock at the door to my grandparents' side of the house. Since he and Nanny had to shout to be heard over the radio, I didn't miss a word they said.

"Your radio is so loud it's causing the house to vibrate," Daddy shouted.

"I'm sorry, Joe," Nanny yelled back. "I'm getting older, and perhaps I'm becoming a little hard of hearing. I don't want to miss my program."

With Pa in compliance, the radio volume wasn't turned down until the end of the half-hour program.

Daddy didn't attempt to argue. Instead, the next day he brought home a small radio and placed it on the night table next to my bed. He told me I could listen to *The Lone Ranger* on my own radio *if* I was in bed before seven-thirty.

However, he neglected one bit of instruction. He didn't tell me when I had to turn the radio off. So often, after *The Lone Ranger* ended, the radio went under the covers with me as I explored the radio band, looking for other programs of interest.

On one memorable evening, I discovered an amazing radio show that gave an abrupt turn to the direction my life was taking. *I Love a Mystery,* with its heavy footsteps, creaking doors, ear-shattering screams, and heart-stopping murders, was not just scary, it was absolutely terrifying. It was exactly what caring parents like mine would never, *ever* allow their children to listen to. At the end of the fifteen-minute episode I lay in bed trembling, frightened of the shadows in the corners of my bedroom, sure that the scrabbling sounds I heard outside my window were those of a crazed murderer. I whimpered to myself. When I fell asleep I had nightmares.

I loved every minute of that radio program, and during all the years it was on I tried never to miss an episode.

During a visit to our branch library, I accidentally

stumbled across a mystery novel written for children. Although I read eagerly and avidly, until that time I had had no idea that mystery stories could also be found in books. I was thrilled. What an exciting way to write! What a marvelous way to tell a story! The mystery novels for children that I found and devoured were not as nerve-shattering as *I Love a Mystery,* but the books filled my need for breath-holding suspense.

At that early time in my childhood I promised myself that someday I would write books and someday I, too, would become a mystery writer.

Chapter Three

I loved listening to my parents and grandparents tell stories about when they were young. I was always eager to hear a Joe story or a Margaret story or a Matt-and-Hattie story. Instead of the names I knew them by, their given names transferred them into a world that existed before mine, a world in which they became the leading characters in their own stories.

I thought how lucky my mother was when she was young to have shared a bedroom with her aunt Gussie. Gussie owned a candy store and made hand-dipped chocolates. She left for work very early in the morning to make the candy and returned late in the evening after she had closed the store. Margaret didn't see much of her aunt, except on Sundays, but each morning when she awoke, she found that Gussie had left a little gift bag of chocolates for her.

My father told about his Irish mother, Mary Elizabeth Lowery, dashing from the restraining arms of her family back into their burning house in the middle of the night. She appeared at an upstairs window, flinging into the darkness something that smashed on the ground. When she stumbled out the front door, her family pulled her to safety and scolded her. What was so important that she had to risk her life to save it?

"The alarm clock!" she answered with surprise. "Without the alarm clock, we'd all oversleep, and you'd be late to your schools and jobs!"

Some of the tales scared me a little, like Daddy's account of the night job he hated when he was a senior in high school. As he described his duties as night watchman in a mortuary, I easily visualized him making his rounds, his only companions the dead bodies waiting to be buried.

One of the family stories that impressed me the most had to do with Nanny—Hattie—when she and Matt had been married about eighteen years and lived in Chicago.

I don't know at what point in their marriage Matt decided to bring his father to live with them, but it was probably not too long after he and Hattie had married. In hushed tones, Mother solemnly remarked that her grandfather, Nicholas Meyer, had become an alcoholic and could not work.

Nicholas lived with his son Matt and his family, but he refused to communicate with any of them. Through the years he never spoke a single word to Hattie or to my mother. Stubbornly, he wouldn't learn English, and the few words he did mutter were in German, translated as "those bad boys," when my mother's younger brothers, Al and Vincent, came near. According to Mother, Nicholas Meyer was a very mean old man.

Each morning Grandpa Meyer would rise early, dress, and go downstairs to the kitchen. He'd take his place at the table, where Hattie was already busy preparing breakfast. He'd grasp his fork in his left fist and his knife in the right and bang them up and down on the table until his food was placed in front of him.

When Mother was seventeen, Hattie became very ill. There were no miracle medicines to rely on at that time, and nothing the doctor prescribed seemed to help. Hattie continued to weaken. Finally, one morning the doctor called Matt into Hattie's room. "I'll tell the children to come in and say goodbye to their mother, and then I'll leave," the doctor said. "There is nothing more that I can do."

Matt held Hattie's hand and cried as the three children came into the room.

Hattie roused herself enough to ask what time it was, and when Margaret told her, she said, "Did you get Grandpa his breakfast?"

"No," Margaret answered. "Grandpa didn't get up."

Hattie opened her eyes. "That's not like him," she said. "Go to his room and find out if he's all right."

Margaret knocked at Grandpa's door, and when he didn't answer, she entered the room. She couldn't rouse him, so she went back to her mother and said, "Mama, I think Grandpa is dead."

Hattie immediately struggled to a sitting position, wrapping her arms around Matt to comfort him. Then, being practical, she said, "There's so much we have to get done." From that moment she began to improve, and a few days later she was well enough to be on her feet again.

I wish that when I was young I had asked my parents and grandparents to tell more and more stories about their lives before I became part of them. I wish I had listened intently so that I could remember each and every word. I wish I had written their stories to keep forever.

There are so many wishes for what might have been. Wishes play a big part in the making of a writer.

Chapter Four

It's not likely to shock anyone to learn that when I was about five or six I didn't always pick up my toys or hang up my clothes. It was much more fun to run outside and play, or climb into a high branch of our next-door neighbor's fig tree to read *Five Little Peppers* or *A Child's Garden of Verses,* two of my favorites.

Every action has a reaction, and my mother's reaction when I was not as tidy as I should have been was to recite a certain poem to me.

Margaret Lowery, my mother, was an energetic person with great leadership qualities. She had waited seven impatient years to have a child, so when I came along she became highly active in the Los Angeles Mothers' Educational Center. This was composed of a group of women whose intention was to search for the most perfect and modern way to nurture, guide, and discipline their children. Apparently, reciting this poem made their list of recommended activities.

I don't remember the title of the poem. I doubt I want to. But it began, *"I love you, Mother," said Little Nell. "I love you more than tongue can tell."*

When I was grown, I came across this poem in a library collection and for the first time learned the rest of it. As I had heard many times, Little Nell told her mother she loved her. But there was more. After Little Nell's declaration of love, she ran outside to play.

Little Nell had a sister, whose name was Little Nan. Little Nan didn't go out and play. She told her mother she loved her, then swept the floor and picked up her clothes and did the dishes. The poem ended with a question: Which little girl loved her mother best?

When I was young I didn't get the message. I didn't listen to the poem beyond the opening lines because when my mother began to recite it, I heard the words like this: *"I love you, Mother," said Little Nell. "I love you more than Tunkentel."*

Immediately, my mind was drawn to Tunkentel. What a wonderful, exciting name! No first or last name. Just one name—Tunkentel. With a name like that, he couldn't be human. He was most likely a troll who sat under a bridge and ate billy goats gruff and stray cattle and chickens and maybe a farmer or two.

But why did this troll named Tunkentel love Little Nell's mother?

What if at one time in the past the villagers had been terribly unkind to Tunkentel—all except for Little Nell's mother? *What if* he had cut his ugly big toe on a rock and had gone looking for help, and she had cleaned and bandaged it? *What if* she had then sent him home with a bag of chocolate cookies?

What if Tunkentel, many years later, decided to leave his home under the bridge and munch his way into the village? The villagers were terrified and ran away—all except for Little Nell's mother, who faced Tunkentel and encouraged him to return home. Deep in his strange troll mind was a memory of this kind and brave woman—who had once again brought chocolate cookies—so Tunkentel lumbered back to the bridge, thereby sparing the villagers.

Or . . . *What if* Tunkentel was not really a troll at all, but a prince who had been put under a spell by a horribly mean witch?—a prince who needed someone kind and pure of heart to break the spell. Enter Little Nell's mother, who learned how to break evil spells from her grandmother, who just happened to be a *good* witch.

Or . . . *What if* Tunkentel was a wizard in disguise who needed a good and loving helper in order to overthrow the evil king who . . .

Each recital of the poem brought forth in my mind a new dramatic possibility involving the troll Tunkentel. I never did get the message my mother was attempting to give me, but I began a lifetime of *what if*s that have led me into story after story after story.

*What if*s are the keys that unlock the door to imagination. They're free. They're plentiful. I used them to open the door wide, and I ran right in. You, of course, can run in, too, whenever you decide you'd like to.

Chapter Five

During my elementary school years I was never fond of arithmetic. I groaned over my homework in addition and subtraction. I often thought that the time I wasted memorizing the multiplication tables would be much better spent blissfully lost in a book of fiction. With that attitude, needless to say math wasn't my best subject.

When I had trouble with my homework in arithmetic, I went to my father. As an accountant, he was the family's expert in math. He would explain the concept of the problems and the method of solving them, and I would then do my homework.

Often I became stuck on one or two problems. Daddy wouldn't work them for me or even give me hints. He'd go over the process, and then he'd say, "Think about them when you go to bed. Tell your mind to work on them. It will do this while you're asleep. In the morning, when you wake up, you'll be able to solve the problems."

I took him at his word. I would read over the two or three unsolvable problems just before I turned off my bedside light, and in the morning—just as Daddy had promised—the solutions would be there. My math grades improved immediately.

Later, when I had grown up, I was fascinated by scientific magazine articles that claimed we use only ten percent of our brain. *That covers the conscious, thinking part of our brain,* I thought, *but what about the part that works while we sleep?* If this were an extra part, and we could use it, too, I'd take advantage of it. I didn't want to miss out on a thing.

From that time on, just before I fell asleep, I'd often think about scenes in a story I was writing, or a problem in a plot that I couldn't seem to solve, or a character, or a missing ingredient, and I'd say to this mystical part of my brain, "Work on it." Usually I'd awake with the answer, or I'd find it the moment I sat down at my typewriter and began to write.

In the 1970s a number of self-help books were published that attempted to explain what was called the unconscious, subconscious, even supraconscious parts of our brains, giving more detail to a process with which I was very familiar.

At this time I had an unusual experience that convinced me that my subconscious mind was on the job. I began to write my second young adult mystery, *The Séance.* I had written only a few chapters when I was interrupted by a number of other projects that demanded immediate care.

"You work on it, I can't," I told my subconscious mind, and put the manuscript aside.

A few months later I was baby-sitting Melia, our first grandchild. To help her get to sleep for her afternoon nap, I lay on the bed with her, singing lullabies. Soon after she fell asleep, I did, too.

I dreamed that the door to the bedroom opened and a group of people filed in. They stood at the foot of the bed, looking at me.

They were easy to recognize. I knew them as the characters I was writing about in *The Séance*.

"I wish she'd get back to our story," one of them said. "She's put us off for too long."

Another character shook his head and looked at me sadly. "It's because she hasn't worked out some problems in the story yet. I think she's procrastinating."

"Why?" someone asked.

"Because she's wrong about me," a character spoke up. "She thinks I'm the murderer, but I'm not. She doesn't realize that yet."

At that moment Melia stirred and woke up. I woke up, too, fascinated by what my subconscious mind had done for me. I wished I had heard more in my dream and wondered if my characters had other messages for me. If they did, I'd have to get busy and find them myself.

The next day I began working once more on the story. The character who had claimed to be innocent had been right. I soon discovered the identity of the real culprit and eagerly finished my manuscript.

I told my father, "Remember when I was in the second grade and you taught me to use my subconscious brain to solve problems while I slept? You were way ahead of your time."

He laughed and said, "It wasn't my idea. My second-grade teacher taught the process to me."

Perhaps over the generations a few people learned and taught that technique. Perhaps it was something instinctive—especially for writers. Recognizing the subconscious mind and putting it to work is one of the best things a writer can do to help with the long, difficult, and totally satisfying occupation called writing. Believe me, there are many days in which a writer needs a great deal more than that recognizable ten percent of the brain!

Chapter Six

From the time Katie McGowan, our youngest granddaughter, could talk, her world was shaped by dialogue. Her baby spoon and fork would carry on a conversation, sometimes joined by salt and pepper shakers. Dolls would chat with stuffed bears, a rosebud in a vase would have a spirited conversation with a paperweight, and an oak leaf would mother an acorn. Life was story. And story was dialogue.

I attribute this verbal approach to the world to heredity. As a child I was exactly the same.

As a Christmas surprise my father, whose hobby was woodworking, built a two-story dollhouse with a pitched roof and a balcony at one end. My mother wallpapered and painted the rooms and supplied the house with furniture and dolls to fit. As more dolls were added, they became an odd assortment. Some were wooden, with bright red smiles and lacquered hair; some were glass-eyed breakable china, with an occasional chip off a tiny nose or foot. A few, such as a molded lead cowboy with chaps and spurs, drifted into the collection. Some I created from odds and ends, like Popsicle sticks and pipe cleaners, to serve as character actors in my countless stories.

When I began creating stories for my dollhouse, my sisters were too young to know or care what I was doing, but as they grew beyond the toddler stage, they'd often sit and watch intently, listening to my doll characters perform their stories.

My audience quickly expanded. Neighborhood friends who had come to play would discover a show in progress. They'd plop down cross-legged on the rug in front of the dollhouse to watch. It wouldn't be long before the doorbell would ring and a couple of kids would ask, "Mrs. Lowery, is Joan going to make a show?"

Often when a friend of Mother's came to visit, her children would be directed to the dollhouse.

"Joan, put on a show," Mother would say, eager to get the children settled so the grown-ups could talk without interruption.

I put no time constraints on my dramas; although some of the plays were short, others could go on and on until we were called to meals or the little kids had to leave to go to the bathroom.

Mother would say to the audience members, "Time's up. Dinner's ready. Come back tomorrow at three o'clock after school." Or even, "We're having guests tomorrow, so please come Monday after three, and Joan will finish the show."

I didn't mind the interruptions. I was an eager, willing dramatist with a ready-made audience. Could any situation have pleased a writer more?

Even though I was young, I knew that a restless, wiggling audience needed to be captured immediately, so I always began my stories with action. Something exciting happened. Something suspenseful. Something that would keep kids in their seats to find out what would take place next.

In my dollhouse dramas there could be no narrator, no explanation, no description. I had only the stiff-bodied, expressionless dolls to tell my stories. But I had *dialogue*.

Dialogue—including my tone of voice—had to tell the entire story. Dialogue opened the first dramatic scene, and dialogue was responsible for the closing line of each play. I had to grab my audience's attention and hold it, and I had to do it with dialogue.

So the opening of my plays would go something like this:

Two girl dolls are seated in the living room as the play begins. One walks to the window and back to her chair. Then she walks to the window again.

BETTY: (cross voice) *What's the matter with you, Mary Jane? Can't you sit still? I'm trying to read.* (I threw in a lot of sibling banter. It was understood by everybody.)

MARY JANE: *Didn't you hear that strange sound, Betty?* (Right off the bat, both names have been established, and something has been said that piques the interest of the audience.)

BETTY: *Hear what strange sound?*

MARY JANE: *That kind of scratching, scrabbling noise, like someone's trying to get inside our house.*

BETTY: (jumps up from her chair and joins Mary Jane at the window) *I knew we shouldn't have stayed in this mountain cabin by ourselves. Summer's over. Everyone's gone back to the city.*

MARY JANE: *Don't blame me. Staying here another week was your idea. You kept saying you wanted to stay in the mountains long enough to see the first snow.*

BETTY: (holds up a hand) *Shhh! Listen. I heard that scrabbling sound, too. I think it's on the roof.*

MARY JANE: (whispers) *Maybe it's an animal.*

BETTY: *Maybe it's a hungry bear.*

MARY JANE: *It's not a bear. Bears hibernate. We're just scaring ourselves. I wish we hadn't listened to the kids at the boat dock talking about the weird monster who lives in the mountains.*

BETTY: *I didn't pay any attention to them. I don't believe in monsters. Besides, they admitted they'd never seen the monster.*

MARY JANE: (scary voice) *They couldn't see him. They said he only comes out after all the summer visitors have gone home!*

I can't remember ever losing an audience, and I learned how important dialogue is in keeping a story alive and moving.

Chapter Seven

During my eighth year Mother decided that the
living room drapes were terribly out of style and would have
to be replaced. These drapes were made of dark red velvet
trimmed with gold fringe, and the matching piece stretched
over the center part of the window was rounded at the top.
After the drapes had been taken down, my creative mother
took a second look at them and thought what a wonderful
covering they'd make for a puppet theater.

Daddy designed and made a folding frame that could
be taken apart and transported in the trunk of our car.
Mother redesigned the drapes to cover the frame and
wrote scripts adapted from traditional fist-puppet plays and
fairy tales. Our entire family helped make and paint fist
puppets, their heads papier-mâché, and Mother sewed their

costumes. Then Mother, my sister Marilyn, and I memorized our parts.

Pat, who was only three at the time, was given a small part, too. Her job was to sit in the audience, a darling doll with a big bow decorating her blond hair. When Punch called out, "Where do you think I got my big red nose?" Pat had to shout back, "From eating red apples!"

Because I loved Pat so much, I suffered for her each time she dutifully yelled out her line and everyone turned and stared at her. Pat was a trouper, although she admitted many years later that she had hated playing that part. Shamelessly, in spite of my love for my youngest sister, I was thankful Pat's job hadn't been given to me and I could work invisibly behind the scenes.

Although the behind-the-scenes work appealed to me more, it didn't always go smoothly. The space was small and crowded with three people, various backdrops, Mother's folding chair, and countless puppets to manage. If I happened to move too close to my five-year-old sister, Marilyn, she would pinch. Marilyn was a cuter, younger near-image of me, but she had definite ideas about what she wanted, and she took no prisoners.

Unless I had puppets on both hands, I'd naturally pinch back, and on a couple of occasions the stage rocked dangerously. I don't know how she did it, but somehow, without missing a line, Mother managed to threaten us into good behavior, and the show miraculously continued without mishap.

For three or four years we were volunteer entertainers with our puppet show wherever there were children—at hospitals, schools, and orphanages. In spite of occasional—and sometimes painful—pinching contests, I enjoyed performing with the puppet show. I loved hearing the children laugh and shout back to Punchinello in our Punch and Judy script, but it wasn't until we performed at a Maryknoll orphanage for Japanese children in Los Angeles that I suddenly realized the magical, transcending power of suspense.

The children in the orphanage shrieked with delight and shouted to Punch when a ghost puppet appeared, attempting to warn Punch about his wicked ways. The ghost would rise at the right of the stage, but Punch would be looking in the wrong direction and miss it. When he'd turn back to where the children were pointing, the ghost would have vanished. As Punch was distracted once more—with the ghost returning—the children screamed and laughed, some of them jumping up and down with excitement.

We were told later by the director of the orphanage that the children did not understand English. But I saw that they understood dramatic action. They understood suspense. Action and suspense. Two important elements writers need to use. I planned to use lots of action and suspense in the stories I'd write so that they'd come alive to readers in every country of the world.

My promise to myself came true. My books are translated from English into many languages so that children in other countries can read them, too.

Chapter Eight

On one damp, drizzly day when I was nine years old, my sisters and I decided to play a game of indoor hide-and-seek. Looking for a new hiding spot where no one would think of searching for me, I hid under my grand-parents' bed.

I made myself comfortable by rolling onto my back. I looked up and was surprised to see, through the uncovered coils of the box spring, half a dozen magazines on Nanny's side of the bed. Since I was an avid reader, intent on read-ing anything and everything that came to hand, I pulled down the magazines and examined them.

True Confessions, Modern Romances, True Love . . . There were a number of magazines of this type, and they were filled with stories. Eagerly I began to read.

My sisters gave up trying to find me and began playing with their dolls, so I read until Mother and Nanny called the family to dinner.

I certainly didn't mean to get my wonderful grandmother into trouble, but some of the words I had read were unfamiliar to me, and later that evening I asked my mother what they meant. Surprised, she asked me where I had heard them, and before long the entire story came out.

Pa, who had emigrated to the United States from Luxembourg when he was only a child, was self-educated, but he avidly read both classic and current literature, and he blamed himself for never having introduced his wife to good literature.

When Nanny was only a child, living in Chicago, her father died, and her mother turned their home into a boardinghouse to support her three children. They all worked very hard. There was no money for higher education for any of them and no one to introduce them to good books.

"It was my responsibility to have supervised my wife's reading years ago," Pa said to my parents, and I heard him tell Nanny that in the evening he would read aloud to her from Sir Richard Burton's translation of *The Arabian Nights: Tales from a Thousand and One Nights*.

If storytelling was on the agenda, I didn't want to miss out, so I arrived in their living room before they did and found a cozy, concealed spot behind Pa's large upholstered armchair.

Pa settled into his chair while Nanny perched gingerly and reluctantly on the edge of the sofa. Pa urged her to relax and enjoy the story. He waited while she settled back a bit, then gave her some background on the selection he was about to read. He said that the wife of the Sultan of India had been unfaithful, so the Sultan had her killed. Each night this untrusting Sultan took a new wife, and in the morning each unfortunate woman was killed.

Nanny raised a disapproving eyebrow at this, but Pa quickly went on to explain that finally the Sultan married a storyteller named Scheherazade, who kept him entertained each night with a story that never ended, continuing from night to night. The Sultan, eager to hear how each episode would end, had to keep Scheherazade alive to find out what happened.

Pa picked up the book, opened it, and said, "This is one of Scheherazade's stories, 'The Porter and the Three Ladies of Baghdad.'" He began to read.

In the story the porter was asked to carry a lady's baggage to her home. A second lady opened the door and was described in this way:

> *Presently the door swung back, and behold, it was a lady of tall figure, a model of beauty and loveliness, brilliance and symmetry and perfect grace. Her forehead was flower-white; her cheeks like the anemone ruddy-bright; her eyes were those of the wild heifer or the gazelle, with eyebrows like the crescent moon; her lips were coral-red, and her teeth like a line of strung pearls or of camomile petals. Her throat recalled the antelope's, and her breasts were like two pomegranates of even size.*

At this Nanny jumped to her feet and cried, "Twin pomegranates! Oh, how rude! There is nothing that vulgar in my magazines!"

She stalked out of the room, and that was the end of her education in classic literature.

However, I quietly latched on to the book and enjoyed it thoroughly . . . as soon as I found out what a pomegranate was.

In reading the tales from *The Arabian Nights,* I discovered and remembered the importance of exciting chapter endings and the withholding of information from readers to make them want to keep reading. Scheherazade used this information to save her life. Today her suspenseful storytelling would earn her membership with other mystery writers in the organization Sisters in Crime.

Chapter Nine

It's always miserable to come down with
the flu, but it's doubly miserable to catch it during the summer. One summer when I was eleven I went to bed so ill I
wasn't even able to read.

On the second morning, still feeling terrible but eager
to be distracted, I turned on my bedside radio and discovered with awe and amazement the world of soap operas.

The soap opera characters were people whose lives were
very different from mine and my relatives' and friends'.
Soap operas then were not heavy with sexual plots, as they
are now. The characters had other problems to solve. Some
problems were inflicted by their relatives and friends, but
most of their problems had been brought on by themselves.

I was fascinated by the unique approaches they used in trying to make sense of their lives.

I was hooked.

All summer long I listened to *Pretty Kitty Kelly, Myrt and Marge, Our Gal Sunday,* and a number of other fifteen-minute-a-day dramas. I still recall the deep, concerned voice that asked at the beginning of *Our Gal Sunday* a question that went something like this: "Can a girl raised from infancy by two grizzled miners in a Colorado mining town ever find true happiness married to an English lord?"

Apparently, she couldn't. At least she didn't find happiness that summer.

As I listened to the daytime radio dramas, I began to realize that there were reasons for what the characters did or didn't do. Later, I discovered that the writer's word for this is *motivation,* but at the time I only learned, with a sense of wonder, that people didn't do a single thing without a reason behind it.

It became obvious to me that the personality and actions of the main character of each story determined the direction the story would take. Because the story belonged to the main character, she—or he—was the most important part of the story.

I also learned from the soap operas to see the action through the eyes of my characters—even the villains, who certainly didn't think of themselves as villains.

As the summer and I progressed through this unusual version of Psychology 101, I realized I should share my newfound knowledge.

Mother and Nanny sewed together and cooked together, and often just had a cup of tea and visited with each other. Situations and problems of friends, relatives, neighbors, and even movie stars were discussed, and usually either Mother or Nanny would comment, "Wouldn't you think she'd have done such and such?" or "Wouldn't you think he'd have known such and such?"

With my fabulous newfound soap opera wisdom, I felt strongly compelled to enlighten Mother and Nanny so that they could share this revelation about how and why people did the things they did.

I interrupted them in the middle of a "Wouldn't you think he'd . . ." as they were discussing one of the relatives, and carefully explained, "You can't expect anyone to solve his problems the way you do."

As they stared at me in surprise I went on. "Everyone has his own reasons for what he does," I said, "and—right or wrong—everyone makes his own decisions. We're all different. We all think for ourselves. Your solutions to problems may be right for you to follow but not right for someone else."

I was impassioned. Before I had finished, I think I even brought in the religious aspect of free will.

Needless to say, Mother and Nanny were not pleased to be enlightened. They sent me off to clean my room. And in their conversations with each other they continued to say, "Wouldn't you think . . . ?" Wanting to stay out of trouble, I kept my opinions to myself.

But I thought long and hard about the soap opera characters. When I was a writer I'd be writing *about* people *for* people, so I needed to know as much as I could about why and how people chose to do the things they did.

From that time on, I was a people-watcher, making mental notes about behavior, body language, and mannerisms. And I listened, not just to what was said, but to the way it was said. I loved unusual speech patterns and idioms and regional dialect. When I was in college I took electives in psychology and sociology, which helped almost as much as people-watching, but in a different way. I was determined to relate to and reach the people about whom I planned to write.

TOP LEFT: At twenty-eight months I was proclaimed the healthiest baby in Los Angeles County, with a blue ribbon to show for it.

TOP RIGHT: At four years old I had my serious moments.

LEFT: Mother and I when I was four. My pale green **velvet** coat was probably the most beautiful coat I've ever owned.

RIGHT: My grandfather, who was retired, spent hours each day with us. At the age of five I could read, but I still liked snuggling in his lap as he read to me.

BOTTOM LEFT: When the pony man came down the street with his pony, camera, and cowboy trappings, my ten-month-old sister, Pat, and I posed together.

BOTTOM RIGHT: Our swimming pool looks pretty rustic, but on a hot day we really didn't care.

This photo appeared in the December 1936 issue of *The California Parent Teacher Magazine,* illustrating the article "All the Family Can Be Puppeteers," written by my mother. Our entire family took part in the creation of puppets and plays.

Mother, Marilyn, Pat, and I with some of the puppets we had made. This photo appeared in the *Los Angeles Times,* accompanying a story about our performances at schools and hospitals.

At the age of nine I was not as serious and reflective as I look in this studio portrait. I loved weed-throwing fights in the vacant lot behind our house.

With my sisters on a family vacation in Lake Tahoe.

My father posed with
me on the day I was
confirmed. I was
thirteen and very much
impressed with this
step into adulthood.

Sixteen and posing in
front of W. C.
Fields's home in
Laughlin Park.

RIGHT: My best friend, Mary Lou, and I in front of the administration and library buildings at Hollywood High School.

BOTTOM: On warm summer weekends Mary Lou and I rode the streetcars to Santa Monica Beach—a great hangout for teens.

I'm posing for a friend who would soon be shipping overseas as a marine. Frequent mail and photographs were important to all the boys who went to war.

I loved being taller than my grandmother and teasing her about it. You can tell by her smile that she accepted teasing with good humor.

I loved the solitude I could find on top of the highest hill in
Laughlin Park.

Bikes could be rented and
ridden along the levee above
the Los Angeles River. It was
a great place, with no traffic.

Mary Lou and I, all dressed up,
ready to attend the
baccalaureate service before our
graduation from Hollywood High.

Chapter Ten

My parents drove a highly unusual car during much of my childhood on 73rd Street, and until they became used to it, some of the neighbors would turn and stare in surprise as we passed by.

Our car was a long black limousine with two folding jump seats between the front and back seats. There were silver vases on each side and a glass window that could be rolled up or down between the front and back seats. The limousine had been previously owned by a famous movie star, character actor Adolphe Menjou, and still carried an air of glamour. My father bought it because it was the only car he could find that held all seven members of our family.

My sisters and I took turns sitting on the jump seats so

that our grandparents could have the comfortable backseat. If Nanny and Pa didn't happen to be with us, and we grew too noisy, Mother, seated in front, simply rolled up the window that separated the front from the back.

These were low-traffic years, so Sunday drives were common. In the spring we rode a short way out of town to walk through fields of wildflowers, and we picked armfuls of blue lupine and California's golden poppies. In the summer we drove for less than an hour to the Long Beach horseshoe or to Alamitos Bay to swim. And in the winter it was a quick trip to Lake Arrowhead in the nearby mountains to play in the snow.

I adopted these settings in the mountains and at the beach for my stories and plays. I didn't have the knowledge to write about faraway lands and countries, so I didn't try to use them for settings. I was aware that my stories would be more believable if I wrote about what I knew. That was easy. Los Angeles had a big backyard, and it was mine.

Chapter Eleven

My life changed abruptly soon after my thirteenth birthday. Pa died, and I missed him terribly. I hadn't always liked being the eldest child in our family, since I was reminded often that as eldest I must "set the example" and "shoulder the responsibility." But now being the eldest gave me consolation. I had known and loved our grandfather the longest. I had thirteen years packed with wonderful memories that I would always cherish.

That summer my parents decided to move across Los Angeles to a much larger home in Laughlin Park, an estate community in the Los Feliz hills, a part of East Hollywood. They bought a large two-story house on an acre of land, most of it planted in hillside gardens of ferns and lilies, roses, and gigantic dahlias. There were six rooms and two bathrooms downstairs and four bedrooms and three baths upstairs. My parents shared one bedroom, my sisters shared another, and Nanny and I became roommates in the third. The fourth very tiny bedroom and bath were designed for a live-in maid, and it wasn't long before Mother hired the first of a short series of household helpers to fill this position.

Mother and Daddy bought the Laughlin Park house from an elderly man, Mr. S., who planned to remarry. His second-wife-to-be refused to move into his house, so he priced it low, eager to make a quick sale. According to the next-door neighbors just up the hill, who couldn't wait to tell us the story, for a number of years Mr. S. and his recently deceased first wife had not had a happy marriage. Mrs. S. had brought her crippled mother and blind sister to live with them, taking care of their expenses on her own, since she was wealthy in her own right.

Mr. and Mrs. S. had made a trip to Bakersfield, California, driving on what was called the Ridge Route, a narrow road with many winding curves. Mr. S. had been speeding, recklessly increasing his speed as Mrs. S. begged him to slow down. He'd lost control of his car and crashed off the road. He was injured only slightly in the accident, but Mrs. S. was killed.

After the funeral, Mr. S. evicted Mrs. S.'s mother and sister, abruptly sending them away—probably to some state welfare institution, the neighbors thought. Although Mrs. S.'s mother and sister had protested that Mrs. S. had provided for them in her will, the will had mysteriously disappeared and was never found.

My parents loved the new house with the shaded patios dripping bougainvillea vines and hanging baskets of fuchsia.

And they praised the rose garden, which had more than a hundred healthy rosebushes. But things changed for me after what I'd heard about the former owner.

I reentered the house, and as I walked alone through the large, empty rooms, I couldn't explain the eerie sensations I felt. A lost will . . . a death that could have been murder . . . If restless ghosts were looking for a place to prowl, this was the house. Maybe it was only my active imagination, but I was sure I could feel the years of sorrow from this unhappy marriage that had seeped into the corner shadows.

None of this bothered my parents, who bought the house because it was beautiful and because it was a great bargain.

After we had moved in, I discovered something curious. The downstairs hallway connected two large rooms at each side of the house. One my parents had designed as an informal den. The other contained a Ping-Pong table and my mother's sewing machine. Two bathrooms, one off each room, were back to back, and in front of the bathrooms, in the center of the hallway, was a linen closet, about five feet deep, with two wide doors that swung closed to meet in the middle.

There was a lock on the outside of the linen closet, and, for no apparent reason, on the inside of the closet were *two* locks. One was a hook and eye and one was a snap lock, both of which could only be operated by someone *inside* the closet.

Borrowing my father's measuring tape, I did some sleuthing. "There's a space about seven or eight feet wide and at least ten feet deep behind the closet," I pointed out.

"That's where the plumbing from the bathrooms would be," Daddy said.

"I allowed for the plumbing," I told him. "Besides, how much space can a few pipes take? I think there's a room hidden back there."

Mother rolled her eyes. "There's no reason for a hidden room."

"There's no reason for the closet to be locked on the inside," I countered. I was eager to see this hidden room. "Just think," I said, "the room might hold, at the least, a missing will. Or at the most . . . well, the neighbors weren't sure what happened to Mrs. S.'s mother and sister. Why don't we take out the shelves? Why don't we find out if the back of the linen closet is false and there's a room behind it?"

"Don't be silly," Mother said. She glanced nervously at the closet. "I've just finished unpacking the sheets and towels and tablecloths and filling all those shelves. I'm not taking everything out just because you have an overactive imagination."

"I'll do the work. I'll take everything out myself, and I'll put it all back," I promised. "If there are ghosts, we should lay them to rest."

"No," Mother said. "And that's final." She began to look frantic. "I don't want to hear one more word about secret rooms or dead bodies or ghosts."

Later, I caught Daddy with the measuring tape, double-checking my figures. He seemed a little embarrassed as he looked up and saw me, but he said, "There does seem to be a good-sized empty space in there, but let's not worry your mother about it. Okay?"

"Why?" I asked complainingly.

"Because," Daddy said. "Just because."

I was sure I knew why. Mother loved her new house, and she didn't want it tainted with anything even the least bit mysterious.

Six years later, one of our near neighbors, the movie star and comedian W. C. Fields, died, and his sprawling mansion was listed for sale.

Mother returned from a walk in the neighborhood and said to us, "The realtor is holding an open house, but no potential buyers are on hand. Walk up the hill with me. We'll tell the realtor we're just nosy neighbors. I'd love to get a peek at the inside of that mansion."

Equally curious, Pat and I went with Mother and met a realtor who was alone and bored. "Come in," she said. "I can at least show you around the first floor."

As we walked into the beautiful wood-paneled entry hall, she stopped us and said, "Let me show you something unusual."

She pressed a button that was hidden within the paneling, and one panel slid open, revealing a room about eight feet by ten feet with a door at one side. "This house was built during Prohibition," the realtor explained. "This hidden room was used to hide the liquor. That door leads to a stairway that exits the property on the street below. It was planned so that if the house was raided, the bootlegger could easily make his getaway."

Our house had also been built in the twenties. Perhaps the mysterious space I had discovered was a similar room, once used for hiding liquor.

Tentatively, I brought up the idea, but Mother was quick to squelch it. "That's nonsense," she said. "First you thought there were dead bodies, then ghosts, and now you're talking about bootleggers. We do *not* have a hidden room in our house, and I don't want to hear another word about it."

I realized I'd made a big mistake in the beginning by blurting out my guesses about dead bodies or ghosts. If I had pointed out only the space itself, Mother might have allowed Daddy and me to investigate it. Now I'd never know whether there was a secret room or what might be inside it.

I had gathered some of the elements of a good mystery: measurements that didn't add up, suspicious characters who had lived in the house, and a missing will. But my motivation was nothing more than curiosity—not strong enough for any story—and the adversary who stood in the way of my investigation was my very own mother.

I consoled myself with the hope that at some time in the future, another owner might remodel the house and discover the secret room and its mysterious contents. I might have been denied the right to solve the mystery, but at least I hadn't lost the element of suspense.

Chapter Twelve

My childhood was generally a happy time. I studied, I played, and I read more books than would be possible to count.

Books were like popcorn, and I gobbled them. Each week Mother took us to our branch library, and I checked out the maximum number allowed, even adding some to Mother's list.

There were books I had never read that beckoned me, teased me, tempted me. I scooped up armfuls, reading every chance I got. Even when Mother said, "You absolutely must stop reading and go outside and get some fresh air!" I'd sneak a book outside and keep reading. And at night I read under the covers with a flashlight.

I didn't know it at the time, but I had plenty of company. I have never met an author who didn't love to read.

After we moved across the city, we had a new branch library to visit—the Hollywood library on Ivar Street. When I entered it I walked across the aisle from the children's room into the adult room.

Often I'm asked what young adult books I read when I was a teenager. My answer is none. There weren't any. No one thought of writing or publishing books with teen characters and issues that would appeal to teenage readers, until Nat Hentoff wrote *Jazz Country* and S. E. Hinton wrote *The Outsiders* in the 1960s.

I read the mystery novels written by Agatha Christie and Ngaio Marsh. I read Raymond Chandler's mysteries because they were set in my own Los Angeles. I read humor and biographies and California history. And sometimes, in my eagerness to know why the world was in such a horrible state, I read nonfiction about the world situation.

"Are you sure your mother will want you to read this book?" the librarian asked as I checked out Jan Valtin's *Out of the Night*, which dealt with Nazi atrocities.

"Oh, yes. She wants me to broaden my mind," I answered.

The librarian sighed as she stamped the due date on the card at the back of the book. "If I were you, I wouldn't read it," she said.

Was she right? The book contained such horrifying descriptions, I soon wished I hadn't read it. Yet I knew I needed to better understand why our country had to go to war to stop the terrible things the Nazis were doing. It was important for as many people as possible—including me—to know the facts.

I knew that reading is the major key to learning, but I also used reading to fulfill my needs for fun and romance and mystery and excitement and deep satisfaction. Even with the precollege course I was taking, I managed to read my own choice of books as well. Classic and contemporary, fiction and nonfiction—they made a good mix. I saturated myself with my favorite authors' various styles and techniques, learning from the very best.

Chapter Thirteen

Dora was Nanny's fifth cousin and lived with
her husband, Ed, in nearby Huntington Park. Overly round
and rouged, Dora was pleasant and friendly with an ever-
ready smile and a halo of short, permanently waved gray
curls. Best of all, Dora had a talent none of the rest of us
had. Dora could communicate with the dead.

Ed, on the other hand, was a gruff, meat-and-potatoes,
no-nonsense person, muscular and sun-weathered as dark as
my second-best brown oxfords.

Dora and Ed eagerly accepted every invitation to our
family's big Sunday dinners because Nanny was a truly great
cook.

Each Sunday afternoon's feast began with a Jell-O fruit
salad and relish dishes full of sliced celery, carrots, and

olives. These were followed by a large roast of beef with browned potatoes and gravy, string beans, fresh corn cut from the cob, sliced tomatoes, and sometimes creamed pearl onions, a favorite of my father's. There were always fresh yeast rolls, set to rise that morning after eight o'clock Mass, and at least three of Nanny's special fruit pies—peach, cherry, apple, or strawberry-rhubarb, depending on the season. We always had Sunday visitors, and Nanny enjoyed that. Her talent lay in cooking, and she loved an appreciative audience, invariably urging them to "have a second piece of pie."

Dora always ate with a healthy appetite, so it was hard for me to believe that she had been quite ill a few years before—so ill that her doctors didn't know how to help her.

However, as Nanny had told me, a friend brought a spiritualist to pray over Dora, and she was cured. Dora was so fascinated with the man's religion, which was called "spiritualism," that she studied it and became a spiritualist herself.

Any type of fortune-telling, psychic reading, or public visitation with the dead, unless it was in conjunction with a church service, was against the law at that time in California. So Dora opened her own church in Huntington Park; she became a spiritualist minister, and her church thrived. She loved to go into trances and believed that a messenger from the next world inhabited her body and could speak through her.

Ed obviously loved Dora, but he had little patience for her so-called dealings with spirits. He enjoyed repeating his story about an incident during a severe earthquake that took place in Los Angeles on March 10, 1933.

According to Ed, Dora had spent the two previous

Sundays preaching about the next world and how she looked forward to entering it. "I'm not afraid of death," she had told her congregation. "I welcome death."

But at 5:54 P.M., when the first and strongest jolt hit, Dora raced out of her house and dropped to her knees in the middle of the street. Raising her arms to the heavens, she shouted, "I didn't mean it, God! I didn't mean it!"

When Dora and Ed visited us after her church service on Sundays, Dora was often on a roll. That meant we might have a few extra guests no one but Dora could see. Although this made my mother very nervous, it didn't bother me. I thoroughly enjoyed everything Dora told us. I was a sophisticated graduate of soap opera's Psychology 101, and I was fascinated by unusual people.

One Sunday afternoon, soon after we had moved to Laughlin Park, Dora and Ed arrived to have dinner with us. I came downstairs to greet Dora, who was seated on the sofa chatting with Mother.

Mother had begun to tell Dora about one of my activities at school when Dora suddenly raised a hand and said, "Hush, Margaret. Your aunt Gussie is with us."

Mother stiffened and paled and gripped her fingers so tightly her knuckles turned white.

In a soft, breathy voice Dora said, "Gussie is standing behind Joan. Her hands are on Joan's shoulders. She is telling us that Joan will become a writer."

I already knew I would be a writer, and my parents always showed a great deal of support for my writing, but I thought it was kind of Aunt Gussie to show up and offer her encouragement, too.

Writers welcome support, no matter where it comes from. My parents and grandparents were proud of the poems and stories I wrote, but what Dora had said gave me a special confidence in the direction I was taking. It was exciting to have Mother's aunt Gussie, someone outside my immediate family, give her honest, unbiased opinion. Besides, I was well aware that this support came from someone who ought to have a better-than-human chance of predicting the future.

On that day I moved one step closer to becoming a writer.

Chapter Fourteen

On the first day of the fall semester at LeConte Junior High School, I walked onto campus with a feeling of dread. I knew no one. I was miles away from the friends with whom I'd grown up. I wished we hadn't moved. I wished I were home in bed.

Then I met Mary Lou Weghorst. As a new student, too, she was probably as lost and scared as I was, but her smile never wavered. We introduced ourselves, we talked until the first bell rang, and we arranged to meet for lunch. Mary Lou became my best friend forever.

Starting a new school and making new friends is always difficult, but it was especially so during the worldwide turmoil of 1940. Germany's military forces were plundering Europe, and everyone was afraid it would be only a matter of time until the United States would be involved in war. Large defense factories had opened in the Los Angeles area, and people were moving to the city in droves to help build planes, tanks, and armaments.

When I enrolled in ninth grade at LeConte, which included grades seven through nine, I found myself in a homeroom composed entirely of newcomers. The administration, for some reason, had lumped us all together, in essence keeping us apart from the other ninth graders. We were treated like outsiders not only by the kids who had gone to school together from their days in kindergarten, but also by a few of the teachers. However, all of us newcomers were going through the pangs of trying to turn strangers into friends, so in a way being segregated made it easier to make the adjustment to this new school.

I had to choose an elective, and somehow I found myself in journalism class. Mrs. Edna Ammons was our teacher and sponsor, and she soon discovered how much I loved to write. At the end of the first week she appointed me assistant editor of the school newspaper, then set about teaching me the rules of journalism.

"Begin each story with the most important fact," she said. "Get your readers' attention. Grab their interest. Then proceed to tell them the rest of the story—who, what, when, where, why, and how."

I gave what she had said a great deal of thought. Grab your readers. Get their attention. I knew this worked for writing fiction. Apparently it was the key to writing news stories, too.

I had read in a magazine feature story that Ernest Hemingway rewrote the beginning paragraphs of his stories as many as fifty times before he was satisfied.

I knew I could be satisfied with a lot fewer than fifty rewrites, but I began to see the importance of the opening sentences of a story and the equal importance of polishing and perfecting those sentences to capture readers.

I took the lesson to heart and, with strong, intriguing beginning sentences that had been written and rewritten, the stories I wrote for my own enjoyment began to improve.

That year, one of the teachers at LeConte, Mrs. Fern Jones, celebrated a contract from a publisher for a book she had written called *Friday, Thank God!* The publisher was G. P. Putnam's Sons in New York, and her book was scheduled to be published in 1943 under a pen name, Fern Rives.

Some of the other teachers teased her good-naturedly about her future fame as an author. Some teased her about writing under a pen name. But Mrs. Jones had won my total awe and admiration. She had written what would become a real hardcover book. It would be published by a New York publisher. Mrs. Jones would even earn money for what she had written.

She wasn't a famous author. She hadn't lived a hundred years ago. She was a real person, like me. If she could get paid for what she had written, someday so could I.

Chapter Fifteen

Another friend in my homeroom of newcomers
was a girl named Betsy Mills, whose father was Felix Mills,
an orchestra leader for a Hollywood studio.

When Betsy asked about my interests, I told her that I
liked to write poems and stories and that someday I was going to be a writer.

Betsy said, "And someday I'm going to compose music.
Let me see some of your poems."

She read a few of them, then said, "Let's collaborate and
write the senior class song."

A notice had been posted, to which I had paid little attention, aside from making sure that it was included in the
school newspaper: One of the English teachers was judging

the annual contest among ninth grade seniors for the class song, which would be printed in the spring yearbook.

"Okay," I said. "Let's do it." And Betsy and I got busy.

For the next few days she'd hum bits of the melody, which had a great beat, and I'd write lines to fit. Finally we had what we thought was a terrific song.

We performed our song for Mrs. Ammons, who beamed as she heard us sing it. "That's the best class song I've ever heard," she said. "It deserves to win." She told us to visit immediately the teacher who was judging the contest and present our song to her. "Come back and tell me how you did," she added.

The judge didn't exactly scowl at us, but with a look as though she'd tasted something bad, she said, "I think we already have our winner. And *she's* not a new student. This is her third year as a straight-A student at LeConte."

"We can't help it that we're new to Hollywood," Betsy said.

"And the deadline for the contest isn't until after school today," I reminded her.

"Mrs. Ammons told us to sing our song for you. She's waiting to hear about it," Betsy insisted.

Before the teacher had a chance to object, Betsy and I went into our song. A few people stopped outside the open classroom door, listened, and began to clap in rhythm.

When we had finished, the teacher looked grim, but she said, "I'll deliberate and announce my decision tomorrow."

I don't know with whom the judge deliberated, but the next day we were told that she had decided in favor of *two* senior songs.

When an assembly was held and the school orchestra played both songs, everyone liked Betsy's and mine better.

We weren't surprised. We didn't even mind that there were two senior school songs. We didn't mind competition. We were preparing for futures in which there would always be competition. Writers have to keep trying. They have to compete.

When the yearbooks came out, however, we couldn't help feeling extra proud of our accomplishment. The straight-A student's song was published on the back page of the yearbook. The song Betsy and I had written was published on the front page.

During the first part of the semester Mrs. Ammons had told me, "A writer must always have faith in herself. If you don't believe in yourself, no one else will."

I took to heart what she said and never forgot it.

Chapter Sixteen

After graduating from LeConte, Mary Lou
and I attended Hollywood High, taking with us all our
teenage insecurities and worries and joys and excitement
and fears and hopes and dreams.

The administrators at Hollywood High used an unusual
system of registration for classes. Each student signed up for
one of three programs, academic, secretarial, or vocational,
and was given a list of the classes required for that particular course for graduation.

On the first day of each semester, newspaper-sized
sheets were handed out, and we sat on the grass, the steps
of the buildings, or the benches in the quad—wherever we
could find a seat—and made out our schedules.

When the first bell rang, we walked—*"Do not run,"* the voice over the loudspeaker warned—to the first class on our list and took a seat. If a student arrived and found that the seats were filled, he either looked for a similar class at the same time or rearranged his schedule.

Not knowing one teacher from another, I assigned myself to a tenth-grade English class taught by Miss Bertha Standfast. At the time I saw only a smiling, middle-aged woman with short, wavy blond hair and round glasses perched on a pug nose. I had no idea that I had just met someone who would make a gigantic difference in my life.

At that time the requirement for students in all English classes at Hollywood High was to write ten themes a semester. This was fine with me, since my favorite class assignment was to write.

Miss Standfast double-graded: one grade for spelling and punctuation and one for writing style. I usually received double A's, but occasionally we had a difference of opinion concerning my choice of verbs.

I have always loved action verbs and thought of them as better descriptive words than adverbs and adjectives, since one well-chosen verb can paint a complete mental picture.

On occasion, though, no one had invented the verb I wanted, so I invented one myself. Someone had to create the language. Why couldn't I do a little of it myself?

In my themes someone would *squeegle* through the mud under a fence, or a harsh laugh would *rackel* in someone's throat.

Miss Standfast would write on my papers, "You can't

make up verbs. Look in the dictionary. There are plenty of very good verbs to choose from."

There were. She was right. I looked for verbs. Action verbs. I realized, even then, that good, strong action verbs made my stories and themes come alive.

I didn't completely give up the idea of making up words, however. One day, as we ate lunch on the lawn in front of the administration building, I brought up a puzzling question to a friend named Nancy Monegan.

"Who makes up slang?" I asked. "Suddenly everyone's saying some new slang word, and before long we read it in our magazines. Then, just as quickly as it comes, it disappears, and new slang takes its place."

Nancy and I looked at each other. "Somebody has to make up slang," Nancy said.

"Why not us?" I asked. "Want to try it?"

Nancy grinned. "Okay. We'll call it our own jabberwocky."

Together we organized our plan. We'd make up a new word or expression for something and use it around campus. We'd then see if others would use it and how long it would take to spread.

I don't remember what our first attempt was, but I do remember that it caught on quickly. It was fun hearing other kids use it, and when Nancy and I later read it in a movie magazine gossip column, we celebrated with a hot fudge sundae at Brown's on Hollywood Boulevard.

We tried other words and expressions and watched them enter the vocabulary of teenagers and magazine writers across the country.

But our days of jabberwocky were soon over. We now knew who invented slang. *We* did. We had proved our point and had influenced the world of our peers. But slang was only a word game. There were more exciting things to do with words, more demanding directions, more complicated challenges. Satisfied that our plan had worked, we quit the game covered in glory.

Chapter Seventeen

Over the next three years at Hollywood High, Mary Lou and I went on double dates together, enjoyed the same movies, sighed over the same handsome male movie stars, rode the Santa Monica streetcar to afternoons at the beach, and listened to each other's problems.

But in our first year of high school, during the Sunday afternoon of December 7, 1941, we were shocked and horrified as we listened to the radio and heard President Franklin D. Roosevelt tell us about the Japanese attack on Pearl Harbor. Our country was at war.

Mary Lou and I did everything we could to help the war effort. Frustrated that we weren't old enough to work at the Hollywood USO or join the navy's WAVES (Women

Accepted for Volunteer Emergency Service) or the army's WACs (Women's Army Corps), we found other ways to become involved.

On Sunday mornings, after early Mass, we sometimes helped serve breakfast to the countless soldiers, sailors, and marines—many of them not much older than we were—who had come to Hollywood on weekend leave. To give them a safe place to stay, cots were set up on Saturday nights in our school's gym, and the girls in the home ec classes, under their teachers' supervision, prepared and served hot breakfasts.

Mary Lou and I often worked in the Red Cross hut on campus after school, cutting cartoons out of donated magazines and pasting them into scrapbooks for the servicemen who were wounded and in hospitals.

We took the Red Cross safety course so that we could help wounded victims if Los Angeles was attacked.

During our first citywide blackout, all those who could remained in their homes. Mother had sewn blackout curtains for all the windows that needed them, but that night, as the sirens sounded their alarm, we turned off all our lights and gathered together on our open upstairs sun porch.

We saw and heard a gigantic metropolis shudder to a stop. All city lights suddenly disappeared, as if a giant had snuffed them out. Automobiles pulled to the side of streets, lights turned off. Not a cigarette glowed, not a house light appeared. Air raid block wardens patrolled the streets, prepared to cite anyone who broke the lights-out order.

A strange thing happened as the metropolis went to sleep. Stars overhead seemed as large and bright as those viewed from darkened mountaintops. They shone over a city that was totally silent. We spoke to each other in whispers, awed by the change we had just experienced.

Almost before we were ready, the sirens sounded again. The blackout was over. We had successfully closed our city, preparing it for possible attack. This was just practice. Sometime in the near future a blackout might mean invasion.

Before I went to bed that night I slipped a long butcher knife from the kitchen under my bed. Maybe we would never be invaded or attacked. But, on the other hand, maybe we would. And if we were, I wouldn't go down without a fight.

Mary Lou and I comforted the girls at school who lost brothers or cousins or friends in battle, and we kept in touch with some of the boys in our classes who enlisted in the navy or marines as soon as they reached the age of seventeen. Mary Lou's father joined the army and, because of his age, was assigned to be a driver for one of the officers. We were grateful he was not fighting on the front lines, but he was away from home, and Mary Lou worried about him.

Los Angeles officials, concerned about the number of men who swarmed to the city on weekend leave, begged the citizens to take the servicemen into their homes for Sunday dinners.

My parents responded immediately. Mother decided that a boy who would go to church while away from home must be a good boy. So she and Daddy would go to Blessed Sacrament Church on Sunset Boulevard after Mass and invite servicemen to come home to be with a family.

Many of the young men who eagerly accepted the invitation were not much older than I, so I'd invite Mary Lou and a few other girlfriends to come to the house. Daddy had painted a shuffleboard court on the driveway and had created an open area at the bottom of our property for tetherball. Inside our house were a Ping-Pong table, a pool table, and a pinball machine that had been fixed so that it didn't require coins.

Often the sailors, soldiers, and marines would come back each weekend until they shipped out, and we'd entertain them by riding the Hollywood streetcar to Los Angeles's historic Olvera Street, with its booths and shops selling spicy taquitos, fragrant homemade candles, and cactus candy. We'd eat lo mein in Chinatown, compete in teams at the huge bowling alley on Sunset Boulevard, and take in a movie.

"Will you write to me?" most of the servicemen would ask before they left for assignment in the Pacific.

"Of course," I'd promise, and I'd dutifully write each week, even though the list grew to eighteen, nineteen, then twenty. Mary Lou did the same.

We weren't alone. Most of the girls we knew wrote stacks of letters to lonely servicemen away from home.

Not all the letters were platonic. Many of the girls in high school found that absence and worry absolutely did make the heart grow fonder. And so I found something I could do.

Every few weeks I'd write a light, romantic oh-how-much-I-miss-you poem. Each time I composed a new poem, I'd take it to school before classes began, and the word would quickly spread. At least half a dozen girls would sit on the steps of the administration building and quickly copy the poem. Then they'd let their friends copy it, and their friends would continue to share it. I sometimes wondered how many lonesome boys overseas were made to feel just a little bit better because of the loving poems their girlfriends sent them.

I felt a strong sense of satisfaction. I was no longer writing just for my own pleasure. I was writing for others, to fill a need.

Chapter Eighteen

Everyone's teen years are hard. Everyone's teen years during World War II were harder. Teenagers were edgy. Adults were edgy. But it wasn't just over the war news. Little things played a strong part. Mother was highly vocal about it.

"Why are you asking for another roll of toilet paper already? Don't you realize that I have to shop at all the grocery stores in the area at least twice a day to try to find toilet paper for sale? There's not enough toilet paper because we're at war!"

"I don't care if you hate squishing orange dye into the white oleomargarine. We can't get butter, and the legislature went along with the dairy lobbyists, so margarine has to be sold white. The military gets all the butter. We're at war."

"Don't ask again if you can learn to drive. Age has nothing to do with it anymore. Gasoline is rationed, and we can't get rubber for tires because we're at war."

At times I wondered if I'd ever be able to please my mother, but I began to understand emotional ups and downs and realize the strong part emotion played in what we both thought and did.

Nanny was not only my roommate, she was also my buddy, but at times I had problems with her, too.

Late one night a suspected Japanese submarine had been sighted off the coast near Santa Monica, and our coast guard had fired at it. Nanny described the action to me the next morning. "I stood right here at our bedroom window and watched the bullets trace red lines across the sky. I was terrified. I didn't know if we were being attacked or we were defending ourselves."

"Why didn't you wake me?" I moaned, unable to believe I had slept through the battle. "This was part of history, and I missed it."

Nanny looked surprised as she answered, "It was a school night. I wouldn't wake you on a school night. You're young. You need your sleep."

I planted and tended my victory garden lovingly. There would be a show of our produce at school, and I was sure that one of my cabbages, which was growing more gigantic by the moment, would win a prize.

The day of the victory garden show arrived, and I went out to cut my cabbage.

Someone had been there before me, and I knew who. We had met one of our neighbors the week we had moved into our house, when my mother found her in our rose garden, cutting an armful of roses for herself.

"It's all right," Mrs. R. had said, smiling and waving her shears. "You have so many roses, we can all enjoy them."

She continued to enjoy a variety of our flowers, along with lemons and cherries from our trees and mint and herbs from our garden.

When I saw that my cabbage had been taken, I stormed into the kitchen. "I'm going to walk around the hill to her house and ask for it back," I insisted.

Nanny shook her head. "You can't do that," she said. "It would embarrass her. It wouldn't be neighborly."

"But it's my entry in the victory garden show."

"Take something else. There are some nice onions in the garden," Nanny said. "You can't be rude to a neighbor."

"She's a crazy neighbor!"

"But she *is* a neighbor, and we must be polite, so take something else to school."

Mother backed Nanny up, and reluctantly, I had to agree. Retrieving the cabbage wasn't as important as sparing Mrs. R.'s feelings. I entered three onions in the show and won only a third place.

Life was complicated enough. Why did I have to keep tripping over questions of right versus wrong? I wanted peace in the world and peace in my home, and I often couldn't find either. Even though I wanted to be totally independent from my mother, my emotions sometimes mirrored hers. My mother sometimes talked about World War I and how she had missed my father and worried about him when he joined the army. Circumstances might be different from generation to generation, but the emotions we felt were the same. We could measure the span of our days through our emotional ups and downs. I began to write about my characters' emotions, and they became more believable and real. Emotions had no boundaries of age or time. The need to love and be loved, the fears, the concerns, the joys, the excitement, and the sorrows didn't vary.

Then I discovered a place of refuge—a grassy spot in front of the three mansions at the top of the hill that crowned Laughlin Park. From this vantage spot on a clear day I could make out the outline of Catalina Island on the horizon, and below I could see the tiny cars and ant-sized pedestrians on Hollywood Boulevard.

Tiny people, tiny problems, and my own problems seemed just as insignificant. The figures I watched were characters in a gigantic citywide play, and I was a character, too. The air was clear and bright, the blue-purple hills of Catalina rose solidly in the far distance, beyond the thin blue line of ocean, and the sun warmed and relaxed my back.

As a writer-to-be I knew that a story is not a story if it doesn't have a problem to solve. Why should the ongoing story of my life be any different?

Chapter Nineteen

For as long as I could remember, I had gone to Sunday Mass, said my morning and night prayers, and tried to obey the laws of God. But as I grew into my teens, questions began popping up like dandelions after a rain.

As I searched for answers and found them, I discovered that I no longer dutifully followed my parents' religion. I had begun to embrace it as my own, and it became not only a comfort, but a challenge. It was not only a gift, it was a responsibility. It helped me make choices and set standards. At times my faith was a lifeline.

When I was fifteen I went horseback riding for the first time with a group of friends. We rented horses at a stable in Griffith Park and set off for an adventure along the bridle trails.

Unfortunately, it had rained for a week, and the horses had not been exercised. One of them spooked at a sudden noise, and the entire group bolted. My horse dumped me in the middle of Griffith Park Boulevard, and I woke up lying on a park bench with someone telling me, "Be still. The ambulance is coming."

I was taken to the Hollywood Emergency Hospital, where I continued to lie quietly on a cot in a room smelling of ether and disinfectant, until finally someone shined a light in my eyes, turned my head this way and that, and said there was nothing wrong with me.

In my dazed state, the nurse who hovered over me looked like the prison matron in a movie I'd seen, so I wasn't surprised when she jerked me out of bed and slammed me down in a wheelchair, grumbling under her breath about kids who pretended to be injured, while she rolled the wheelchair to my mother's car.

"How about my friends?" I struggled to ask. "Was anyone else hurt?"

"They're all fine. You are, too," she snapped.

But I wasn't. At home I continued to lie in bed with a headache so miserable it became a barrier against the rest of the world.

After a week, when the pain in my head didn't abate, my mother took me downtown to the medical group to which my family belonged. The doctor, who at first also thought there wasn't anything seriously wrong with me, finally X-rayed my head. A short while later he came into the room with a serious look on his face. "She has a fractured skull," he said. "We'll keep her in the hospital on her back, with her head propped so she can't move it. Then all we can do is wait to see if she'll recover."

My sister Pat, who was in fifth grade at Incarnate Word Academy, tearfully confided to her teacher that she was so worried about me it was hard for her to think of anything else. The nun who taught Pat's class promised that on Sunday afternoon at two o'clock, when all the nuns in the convent gathered for special prayers, they would pray for me.

On Sunday afternoon soon after two o'clock, in spite of my never-ending headache, I fell asleep, and I dreamed. In my dream my grandfather walked into the room and sat beside me, stroking my forehead. As his strong hand gently moved again and again against my hair, the pain began to lessen. Finally it left completely. Pa bent to kiss me; then without a word he was gone.

To everyone's delight, an hour later I awoke free of pain. The next day, Pat excitedly reported my dream to her teacher.

Because I had had to miss so much school that spring semester, it was necessary to make up two classes in summer school. Geometry II and Spanish II were offered only at the same time at Hollywood High, so I signed up to take the classes at Incarnate Word, which offered to arrange classes to fit my schedule.

The nun who was registering the summer students gave me a long, searching look. "You were healed while we prayed for you," she said.

"Yes," I answered, remembering the thank-you note I'd written to them. "And I'm very grateful to you."

She gave a little wave of her hand, as if to push my gratitude aside. "You received a message from God," she told me. "You must listen and look within yourself. I believe that God wants you to become a nun."

It didn't take long for me to listen or to look within myself. How could I shut myself up in a convent at the age of fifteen? Especially since I had recently discovered that the world was full of good-looking guys.

"Well?" she asked me.

"I'm not sure what message God gave me," I answered truthfully. "Maybe he wants me to become the mother of a bishop."

That was the end of our conversation. She wasn't happy with me. But I was happy with myself, and my faith hadn't suffered.

Later, I began to see that my beliefs, my standards, and my outlook on life were as much a part of me as the color of my hair and eyes, and they influenced what I wrote and how I wrote it. The main characters in my stories, in whole or in part, reflected what I believed and what I liked about the world.

I learned that it is important for authors to connect with their main characters. It is important to like them. My characters live inside my head for many months—sometimes even years. Before I write more than a few notes about my story line, I begin to visualize and understand my main character, choosing the person who's closest to the problem in the story. By the time I'm ready to write, I know my main character as well as I know myself. A little part of her is often a little part of me.

Chapter Twenty

Although I loved my mother very much, I didn't always see life as she did. This was disappointing but not surprising. Most of the girls I knew had the same problem.

At Hollywood High, Mary Lou and I had joined the girls' drill team, and we were thrilled when we were told that our team had been invited to march in Hollywood's Santa Claus Lane Christmas Parade.

It was always a glorious parade, with movie stars riding on Santa's float, and we felt just as glamorous as they did, picturing ourselves marching snappily along in our crisp white cotton uniforms with bright red belts, snug red cotton jackets, and red cloth caps.

A guy in whom I was interested told me he was going to the parade to see me march and asked if we could get together after the parade was over. Since I knew it would be hard to find each other in the huge crowd that was expected, I invited him to meet me at our house afterward. Mary Lou had a date, too, and we were so excited we could hardly wait for the big day.

But two days before the Christmas parade, Los Angeles was hit with a blast of icy weather.

"That little cotton uniform isn't nearly warm enough," Mother told me. "You'll have to wear a coat."

"I can't wear a coat!" I protested. "We're wearing uniforms! We have to look alike!"

Nanny shook her head. "You'll catch pneumonia," she said. "At least wear a sweater."

"I can't!" I insisted.

"Then you aren't going," Mother said in her firmest tone of voice. "We won't let you freeze to death."

"I *want* to freeze to death," I argued. "I want to turn blue and get covered with goose bumps like the princesses usually do on the floats in the Rose Parade."

"Sarcasm won't help," Mother said. But I wasn't being sarcastic. Sometimes, depending on the weather, the Rose Parade princesses' skin did look blue.

Neither of us would give in, and I went to bed in tears, desperately wondering what to do.

In the morning, Mother had come up with what she and Nanny thought was a good solution. "We'll make you a dress out of an old wool blanket," Mother said. "You can wear it under your uniform, and no one will be able to see it."

"I'll look weird."

"No, you won't," Mother said in a voice as firm as a

solid oak door. "You'll wear the blanket dress under your uniform, or you won't march in the parade."

"I'll die of embarrassment," I wailed.

"At least you won't die of pneumonia," Mother answered.

I didn't have a choice. Just before the parade Mother sewed me into the blanket dress, and I tugged my uniform over it.

I felt as if I'd been stuffed into a sausage casing. As the uniform was zipped up with great difficulty and the jacket strained at the buttons, I found myself almost immobile. It was hard even to move my arms, let alone swing them.

"I don't mind being cold," I wailed, but my protests did no good.

When we reached Hollywood Boulevard, where the parade was to begin, I left my bundled-up parents, sisters, and grandmother standing on the sidewalk to watch the parade, and joined our drill team.

A couple of the girls gave me strange looks, but Mary Lou told me I looked terrific and no one could possibly notice that I was also wearing a blanket. The night air was crisp and cold, and a few of the girls were shivering. I envied them. I wished I could shed the blanket dress and shiver, too. But I didn't dare.

Under the glittering tinsel and sparkling colored lights, we marched with precision—and, on my part, with some awkwardness. I couldn't relax and enjoy our team's glory, because I knew all eyes and the cameras of Movietone News were upon us. I cringed inside as I pictured my overstuffed self through the eyes of the guy I liked.

Finally, the parade was over, I found my parents in the

mob of spectators, and we returned home. I had changed into slacks and a shirt before my date reached our house.

"You looked great!" he said as he greeted me. "I couldn't take my eyes off you."

As I stood there blushing, totally miserable, and wishing he weren't trying so hard to be so kind, he said, "You were easy to spot, since you were on the end in the front row."

I blinked with surprise. Front row? On the end? The girl who had that position was as tall as I; we both combed our dark hair nearly the same way, and we even looked something alike—especially in the evening light. If someone watching us didn't have twenty-twenty eyesight . . . Oh, wow! This guy was perfect in every way.

"Thanks," I said, beaming.

Later I told Mary Lou what he'd said. "That's so romantic," she told me. "You could write a story about it."

I tried, but I couldn't make my story sound believable. The girl who was my main character didn't do a thing to solve her own problem, so the ending of the story was pure coincidence. I had learned from all the books and stories I read that readers don't like coincidence. And they don't like main characters who don't have the spunk and intelligence to solve their own problems.

Lots of interesting things happen to people, I decided, but they don't all make good stories. It's a writer's job to know which is which.

Chapter Twenty-one

During each summer after he became auditor of Los Angeles County in 1938, my father attended a statewide convention that was always held in San Francisco.

Mother enjoyed attending the activities planned for wives, such as luncheons, fashion shows, and flower arranging demonstrations, so as soon as I reached my teens, I was given spending money and the care of my sisters.

I had always been good with directions, and I soon learned the layout of the parts of San Francisco we most enjoyed. We'd ride the cable cars to Fisherman's Wharf and eat shrimp cocktails in paper cups—walking cocktails, they were called. We'd stroll up and down the streets of Chinatown, browsing in the fascinating shops. And we'd take the bus to the aquarium in Golden Gate Park and the M. H. de Young Memorial Museum, walking afterward to the Japanese Tea Garden for lunch.

I loved San Francisco, I loved entertaining my little sisters, and I particularly loved the freedom that I had been given to explore.

Each convention ended with a dress-up dinner, complete—for the women—with hats and gloves. Marilyn, Pat, and I were always included. So the summer I was sixteen, an hour before we were to leave our room in the St. Francis Hotel to appear in the banquet room, I dutifully dressed in my short-sleeved black dress—the fashion uniform of the day. I added the traditional string of costume jewelry pearls and white gloves. I stopped, looking hesitantly at Mother, who was brushing Pat's hair.

"Uh-oh," I said.

Mother looked up, suddenly wary. "What does *uh-oh* mean?" she asked.

I tried to seem nonchalant. "Nothing much. It just means I forgot to pack my hat."

Mother dropped the hairbrush. "You couldn't forget to pack your hat! You're old enough to be responsible!"

"I *am* responsible. I just happened to forget it," I said.

"You can't go to the dinner if you're not dressed properly. And you aren't dressed without a hat."

I glanced out the window of our hotel room, across a corner of Union Square to I. Magnin's elegant store on the corner of Geary and Stockton. On the sidewalk next to the building rose a rainbow of color—one of the large street-corner flower stalls for which San Francisco was famous. But its beauty did nothing to dispel the dark mood in our hotel room.

"I could run over to I. Magnin and buy a hat," I quickly suggested.

"No, you can't," said Mother, who never bought anything unless it was marked down in a fifty-percent-off sale. "We couldn't afford an I. Magnin hat." She looked at her watch, her voice rising. "Besides, all the stores closed at least half an hour ago."

She was close to panic. "What are we going to do? We can't leave you up in the room, and you can't go to the banquet if you're not properly dressed! You know that your hat is as important as your stockings and shoes. How could you be so careless?"

I took another look out the window and got an idea. "I'll be right back," I told her. I snatched up my handbag and ran out the door.

When I arrived at the flower stall it was empty of customers and the flower vendor was getting ready to close for the evening.

Out of breath, I poured out my story and asked, "Could you possibly make me a hat out of flowers?" I held out all the money I had—three one-dollar bills.

He studied me. "Your mama's real mad at you. Right?"

"That's right," I said. "I have to come up with a hat."

He grinned, weather-beaten wrinkles crisscrossing his cheeks. "A pretty girl like you needs a pretty hat," he said. "Sure, I can make you a hat."

He chose a handful of pale aqua carnations, and with florist wire and a bit of black netting, he soon fashioned a crown of flowers with a tiny black veil.

I pinned it on with two bobby pins and peered into my pocket mirror. The hat was gorgeous, and I felt gorgeous, too.

"The color makes your eyes sparkle," the vendor said. "You are beautiful, so you are happy. Happy endings are the best. Right?"

"Right," I answered. "Happy endings are always the best."

I thanked him profusely and hurried across the square to the hotel and up to our hotel room, where Mother stared at me with her mouth open.

"Now I have a hat," I told her.

Not yet ready to give in, she said, "It's not a hat. It's flowers."

"Lots of hats have flowers," I told her. "Mine just happen to be real."

During the evening, quite a few people complimented me on my beautiful hat, and Mother thawed a little bit.

But I glowed. The flower vendor was right. Happy endings are the best. I envisioned an entire lifetime of happy endings—my characters' and my own.

Chapter Twenty-two

Mother had been a kindergarten teacher, and she decided that I should follow in her footsteps.

But Miss Standfast, whom I chose as my English teacher every single semester through my three years of high school, sometimes talked to me about my love of writing.

Then one day she assigned a theme in which we were to emphasize sensory perception.

As a couple of the guys in the class groaned, Miss Standfast said, "Don't let the words 'sensory perception' worry you. They simply mean, tell us how things sound and taste and look and feel and smell as you use description in your themes."

I gave the idea a few moments of thought, then decided to write about my eleven-year-old sister, Pat, and Mary

McKenzie, a girl close to Pat's age. Because of the war, Mary had been sent from England to stay in safety with her aunt and uncle, who lived next door to us. Pat had blond curls that bounced as she walked and smiles for everyone; Mary had long, dark hair, usually neatly twisted into braids, and she had the serious demeanor of a child who had been separated from her parents and didn't know whether they were safe or not while England was being bombed by the Nazis.

I worked hard on my theme, using sensory perception wherever I could. When my paper was returned, Miss Standfast had written on it, "You are a writer. Come and talk with me after class."

I did, and she told me, "Don't let go of your talent. When you move on to college, develop your writing skills. The local universities don't offer majors in creative writing, but you can major in journalism."

I brought the idea up with my parents, and the result wasn't too pleasant.

Mother was shocked and asked, "Do you mean you don't want to be a teacher—like me?"

Daddy frowned. "I don't want you to be a newspaper reporter," he said. "They drink."

"I'm not going to drink. I'm going to write," I answered.

"No one makes money as a writer," Mother said. "As a teacher, you'd have a nice, steady job."

"But I love to write."

"You'd love to teach, too. You haven't tried it. Don't turn down the idea until you've tried it."

"But I'm beginning my senior year," I insisted, "so I have to decide what I'm going to major in when I begin college. I want to major in journalism."

"You'll be attending the University of Southern

California. Does U.S.C. offer a major in journalism?" Daddy asked.

"Yes," I said, still excited by Miss Standfast's faith in me. "And that's what I want to major in. Someday I'm going to be a published writer."

Mother made a little noise that sounded something like a sob. "Aren't you the least bit interested in our good advice?"

I tried to placate her without giving up. "It *is* good advice, and I appreciate it," I said. "You loved being a kindergarten teacher, so you loved your job. Don't you see that I love writing, and I want someday to have a job I love?"

Daddy nodded, his decision made. "We'll let you major in journalism, if you're going to insist," he said. "But we won't allow you to become a newspaper reporter." He lowered his voice and looked stern. "They drink," he repeated.

I had no desire to drink. My desire was to write. And now that I had a definite goal in mind, I was eager to reach it.

I began my first semester at the University of Southern California at the age of seventeen, in June 1944, one week after I graduated from high school.

Chapter Twenty-three

To graduate **U.S. Navy** and U.S. Marine Corps officers as quickly as possible, the University of Southern California offered three sixteen-week semesters a year, instead of two. I chose to begin classes as soon as possible instead of taking a long summer off.

On the first day, I brought my lunch in a paper bag, as I had done in high school. I sat on a bench outside by myself, not knowing a single soul at the university, and tried not to notice the strange looks passersby were giving me. Brown-bagging your lunch to college was not the thing to do. Nobody had invented the term "cool" yet—not even Nancy Monegan and me—but I was decidedly not cool.

I managed to survive my embarrassment, eating lunch at a drugstore lunch counter off campus until I discovered that the nonmilitary students ate in the student union and in a campus restaurant called the Wooden Horse. And I was soon in great athletic shape—not because I was a member of a sports team, but because my freshman journalism class was on the fourth floor of the student union, where the newspaper offices were situated.

We composed everything we wrote on typewriters, even taking our exams on typewriters. This was fine with me because I had learned to type in seventh grade, and I had discovered a direct line from the creative part of my brain that ran down my arms and came out through my fingers. Composing on a typewriter was always what I did best.

In Journalism 101 I was given the same rules of writing that I had learned from Mrs. Ammons. I knew them by heart and, even though I was a lowly freshman and not eligible to write yet for *The Daily Trojan,* I was eager to work on my journalistic skills.

One afternoon, as I walked up the hill to our house, I picked up our mail, which was delivered to the box at the bottom of the driveway. As I tossed the mail onto the kitchen table, I dropped and then picked up a small magazine called *The Ford Times.* It was a magazine sent monthly to people who had purchased Ford automobiles.

Normally I wasn't at all interested in reading the magazine, but on that particular day I thumbed through it and noticed an invitation to readers to send in short articles about how they and their families used Ford cars.

I sat down at the typewriter, put myself into my mother's shoes, and wrote a few paragraphs about how my husband and I entertained our three young children on short trips in our Ford sedan.

I revised and polished what I had written, then typed a

clean copy with my name and address. I mailed it to the magazine's editor.

About three weeks later, after I had forgotten I'd written the article, I received a letter from the editor of *The Ford Times*. He thanked me for my submission, told me it would be published, and enclosed a check. As I remember, it was for twenty-five dollars.

My legs wobbled, so I quickly sat down, staring in astonishment at the check. I had been paid for something I had written. I hadn't written a book. It was only a short article. But I had been paid. Just like Mrs. Jones. Just like Ernest Hemingway and Agatha Christie and the authors of all the books I'd ever read. And just like the fiction and non-fiction writers in *McCall's* and *Ladies' Home Journal* and the newspaper reporters of the *Los Angeles Times*. I was exactly what I had always wanted to be. I was a published writer!

Epilogue

I had four little children by the time I went to my first writers' conference, in 1961. Afterward, I told my family what I'd heard about writing for children and said it sounded like something I might like to do.

The next day Kathy, who was eleven, and Maureen, who was seven, told me, "Mommy, if you're going to stop writing for magazines and start writing for children, then you have to write a book, and it has to be a mystery, and you have to put us in it."

To please them, I did. *The Mystery of Hurricane Castle* was rejected by the first twelve publishers to whom I sent the manuscript, but the thirteenth—Criterion—liked it, offered me a contract, and published it in 1964. *Young Readers Press* bought paperback rights, and the book was chosen as a selection of the *Calling All Girls* Magazine Book Club, so I knew the first twelve publishers had made a mistake. I hoped they were all very sorry. I enjoyed writing for children so much, I kept going and didn't stop.

Before I sent this manuscript to my editor, my husband read it and complained, "You didn't put me in your book."

"That's because it's about events that had a bearing on my writing from the time I was a toddler through my teen years."

"I met you when you were a teen," he said. "You were nineteen, two weeks away from your twentieth birthday. That should count. And I've always been your best critic and your number-one fan."

I gave in easily. "What you just said is important," I told him. "Every writer needs someone who will read what she writes, then speak the truth. And every writer has discouraging moments when she needs to be told—truth or not—that she's the very best. I'll put you in the book."

And I did.

Whether you want to be published or just write for your own enjoyment, I hope you'll find your own writing niche and love creating with words as much as I do.

JOAN LOWERY NIXON'S TOP TEN WRITING TIPS

Not everyone needs to be published. Not everyone wants to be published. You who do, however, know that writing is not just a talent and an art. It's also a craft with rules to be learned. Just as a musician must learn and practice, so must a writer. Here are some suggestions.

1. Read!

There is never a shortage of good things to read. Whether you're a reader who zeros in on one particular subject or a reader with a wide variety of tastes, find out what is being written and ask for recommendations. Let your librarian and teacher know what you like to read. Talk about books. Ask your friends what they've read that they really liked. The best way to become a good writer is to be a good reader.

2. Write what you know.

Sometimes the setting of a story plays only a minor part, but in some stories the setting becomes more important because it's necessary to the plot. A girl who raises a prize bull has to live on a ranch. A boy who works as a bike messenger will probably ride the busy streets of New York City. Sometimes writers visit and study new places while they're researching stories because they want their descriptions to be accurate. However, mostly they write about places they know well. Your neighborhood is old and familiar to you, but it's new and exciting to readers who live in other states.

Take a good look around you. What makes your house, school, or neighborhood an interesting place in which to set a story?

3. *Show,* don't tell.

A story consists of a series of scenes leading to the climax of the story—the most intense scene of all. Scenes contain the story's action. Through dialogue, action, and visual description, they show what is taking place. Dialogue should sound natural and logical. Sometimes it helps if you read it out loud. Write your scenes through your character's emotions, showing at all times how he feels about what is taking place, and your readers will be pulled into the story, living those emotions with him.

4. Put yourself in other people's shoes.

Try to see the world from different viewpoints, because when you write you'll have to place yourself inside your characters' minds and think the way your characters think. While you're writing, you'll become your main character. Learn as much as you can about her likes and dislikes, her friends, her interests, her beliefs, hopes, and fears. Try to understand the reasons behind your characters' actions so that they'll seem logical and believable. Live with them. Make friends.

5. Trust your characters.

Each story contains a conflict or problem that has to be solved (the plot). The only one who can solve the problem is the person to whom the story belongs—the main character. Sometimes it's tempting to allow an adult or the character's best friend to step in and handle the situation, but writers can't do that. The secondary characters can help, but the final resolution of the problem is up to the main character herself. Let her use the courage and cleverness you gave her when you first dreamed her up. The story belongs to her.

6. Use action!

Toss readers into the action of each story with the beginning paragraphs. Make them want to keep reading. Keep up the action throughout the story, and make sure to include plenty of suspense. Suspense simply means using the elements of surprise, tension, concern, or fear (sometimes in a mystery story) to keep readers guessing, unable to put the book down until the very end.

7. Know your audience.

At some time during your life you've probably listened to a storyteller. Storytellers choose stories to please their audiences. Preschool, intermediate, teen, or adult—each group will hear stories of special interest to them, told in ways they like best.

Writers are storytellers without visible audiences, but they keep their audience/readers in mind. Naturally, writers please themselves with what they have written, but they are also saying to their readers, "I want you to enjoy this story so much you'll ask for another book to read, and another and another." The love of reading, passed from author to reader, is what writing is all about.

8. Learn the rules of grammar.

When I was ten I was given a rhyming dictionary. When I was twelve my parents bought me a thesaurus. In my teens I bought a copy of Strunk and White's *The Elements of Style*. And I have always kept a dictionary close at hand.

Even though we all get instant help from our computers—who hasn't been thankful for the spell checker?—the correct use of language, punctuation, grammar, and spelling is an important part of being a writer.

9. Share your work.

Writers like approval of their work, and they like to be with other writers who share the same dreams. It's fun to know people with the same interests as your own, and it's great when those people listen to your stories, give their advice, and ask for your advice in return.

Many schools offer writing clubs for students, as do quite a few libraries and bookstores. Even meeting sometimes with just two or three of your writer friends can give you the encouragement and help that's needed. You may not have a Dora or an Aunt Gussie in your life, but look for people among your family, teachers, or friends who believe in your talent and are eager to share your interest in writing.

10. Don't be afraid of rejection.

Those of you who want to be published writers should be alert for publishing opportunities. There are magazines that invite young people to submit stories and articles, newspapers that conduct writing contests for kids, and national writing contests of all types, all of which your teachers can help you enter. If your school has a newspaper, yearbook, or literary journal, get involved and contribute your work. Don't be afraid to compete. To be published, you must submit what you've written and take the risk of rejection.

I know from experience that rejection slips hurt. I don't know a single published writer who hasn't received rejection slips. But none of them gave up. I didn't, either.